A CHRISTMAS TAROT
Ghosts of Past, Present, and Future

DINAH ROSEBERRY

Illustrated by CHRISTINE "KESARA" DENNETT

"I will honour Christmas in my heart, and try to keep it all the year.

I will live in the past, the present, and the future. The spirits of all three shall strive within me.

I will not shut out the lessons that they teach!"

—Charles Dickens, *A Christmas Carol*

DINAH ROSEBERRY

A Christmas Tarot

Ghosts of Past, Present, and Future

Illustrated by CHRISTINE "KESARA" DENNETT

Copyright © 2018 Dinah Roseberry and Christine "Kesara" Dennett

Library of Congress Control Number: 2018934115

All rights reserved. No part of this work may be reproduced or used in any form or by any means—graphic, electronic, or mechanical, including photocopying or information storage and retrieval systems—without written permission from the publisher.

The scanning, uploading, and distribution of this book or any part thereof via the Internet or any other means without the permission of the publisher is illegal and punishable by law. Please purchase only authorized editions and do not participate in or encourage the electronic piracy of copyrighted materials.

"Red Feather Mind, Body, Spirit" logo is a registered trademark of Schiffer Publishing, Ltd.

Designed by Danielle D. Farmer
Type set in BauerBodni BT/VTKS Good Vibration/Whitney

Tower card: used with permission by Schiffer Publishing and author Preston Dennett (cover from *Ghosts of Greater Los Angeles* by Preston Dennett)

ISBN: 978-0-7643-5568-4
Printed in China

Published by Red Feather Mind, Body, Spirit
An Imprint of Schiffer Publishing, Ltd.
4880 Lower Valley Road
Atglen, PA 19310
Phone: (610) 593-1777; Fax: (610) 593-2002
E-mail: Info@schifferbooks.com
Web: www.redfeatherpub.com

For our complete selection of fine books on this and related subjects, please visit our website at www.schifferbooks.com. You may also write for a free catalog.

Schiffer Publishing's titles are available at special discounts for bulk purchases for sales promotions or premiums. Special editions, including personalized covers, corporate imprints, and excerpts, can be created in large quantities for special needs. For more information, contact the publisher.

We are always looking for people to write books on new and related subjects. If you have an idea for a book, please contact us at proposals@schifferbooks.com.

Courtesy of Bigstock © Keo, vector file of horizontal elements decoration design, and © Alex Melnik, Religious cross design collection. Isolated on white background. Vector EPS 8

DINAH:
*For my daughter, Angela; her success
is in the cards, and my love for
her spans the Universe.
And for Ari, my "best-est" friend.*

CHRISTINE:
*I would like to dedicate this deck and book
to my son, James, and daughter,
Mudita, who extend the ancestral lineage
of spirits always there communicating
and watching over us all.*

ACKNOWLEDGMENTS

Dinah: A special thank you to friend Christine "Kesara" Dennett for allowing me to partner with her and to display her beautiful (and ghostly!) illustrations. Thank you as well to the brutal (this is a good thing) Schiffer copy editors, Kim Hufford and Peggy Keller; the creative designers, John Cheek and Danielle Farmer; "spirited" Chris McClure in sales; the fabulous customer service team, Pam Braceland, Becky Riggins, and Lindsey Holloran; the perfect overseer, Carey Massimini; Roxy and the warehouse team; and additional senior staff members, Pete Schiffer, Jamie Elfrank, and Jesse Marth—and there are at least twenty more people whom I've not mentioned who made the magic of this deck and book happen. Thanks to all of you!

Christine: I would like to thank my mother, Carolyn Ramos, and sister, Cat Ramos, for continual support in my passions as an artist. I am eternally grateful for the support of my husband, Mark Dennett, in the lean times when I was struggling to gain income for the arts. He has always been understanding and loving. Last, I thank my brother-in-law, Preston Dennett, for being a tremendous influence in my career as an artist for the paranormal community. I would have never known the spiritual connection to the world without his support and publications of my artwork in his books and articles.

CONTENTS

11
INTRODUCTION

The Ghostly Past, Present, and Future Spread.....13

An Oracle, Too.....18

Sample Reading.....19

21
THE MAJOR ARCANA CARDS

0 Fool 22	8 Strength 46	16 Tower 70
1 Magician 25	9 Hermit 49	17 Star 73
2 High Priestess.......... 28	10 Wheel 52	18 Moon 76
3 Empress 31	11 Justice 55	19 Sun 79
4 Emperor.................. 34	12 Hanged 58	20 Judgment 82
5 Hierophant.............. 37	13 Death 61	21 World...................... 85
6 Lovers 40	14 Temperance............ 64	
7 Chariot 43	15 Devil...................... 67	

88
WHAT IF YOU WANT MORE THAN A 3-CARD SPREAD

92
WRAPPING UP

93
RESOURCES

FROM THE CHRISTMAS ANGELS

Christmas is a time that puts people in a place of calm and love. It matters not that it is a religious celebration or that some think it is not, but rather that we—the angels on high—find more individuals to minister to and to care for during this time.

Any form of love can apply throughout the year. Christmas makes this loving task easier and more joyful, and we thank you for taking this journey with your author and illustrator into the world of mystery to find such love.

We are there beside you. Always.

INTRODUCTION

In 1843, Charles Dickens made history—though he certainly didn't know it at the time—by writing what many say is the best ghost story ever written: *A Christmas Carol*. Its ghosts of the past, present, and future enveloped Christmas and the emotions that went with the living and dying of every individual in the world—whether Christian or otherwise. Live wrong, reap the suffering. Live right, reap the gains. Listen to the advice of Dickens' Marley and Marley and their troop of malleable apparitions. It's very simple really: We are all at one time or another mean and miserly Ebenezer Scrooge or kindly day-to-day lifer Bob Cratchit. We each even have a bit of sickly and sorrowful Tiny Tim in us in some uncomfortable way. We marvel during the holidays at the wonderful actors perceiving these famed characters: Alastair Sim, Patrick Stewart, even Kermit the Frog. All have the same effect—they strive to teach us how to live a good life and, therefore, avoid a bad outcome. This story teaches love.

But love is not that easy sometimes, is it? The days come and go with us wondering why things happened or what will happen next. We often don't even know what is clear for our present. Ghosts of these timeslips follow us wherever we go. Some call it synchronicity—others, coincidence—but every time a traveler through life peers into the recesses of the mind, these ghosts permeate and circulate. They have the ability to lead and guide and hide or provide the truth of existence and love.

Looking at Dickens' characters and story lines, it might seem to be vastly historical and not in tune with today's daily turmoil or your personal span of living. There have been others greater than Christine and I who have made these comparisons and have seen the similarities in massive proportions. We won't go there now. With *A Christmas Tarot*, we have used the Christmas ghosts of past, present, and future to connect to the Christmas spirit and magic that dwells in all our souls. There is a way to look inside to interpret your life's path within these pages. Take it to make the best decisions, depending on the angels of Christmas who stand with you every day as you live your life. You don't have to believe in them for them to be there. Often we thank God for that! Still the advice is now available to help you through.

In this Majors-only Christmas deck of 22 cards, even a beginner can manipulate the paths of self-discovery through Tarot interpretations that are personal and catapult you forward toward right thinking—loving thinking. Each card represents a Major Arcana presence in a contemporary ghost depiction. The card will speak to you immediately as you see the connections between Tarot and the images chosen to represent the traditional characters of the deck. There will be a general statement that will reflect closely what you are dealing with when the chosen card is laid down before you. The card will also show a Christmas element chosen specifically for the connection between you and the card, along with its meaning and historical background. There are three meanings that encompass past, present, and future—the most popular quick spread used in Tarot. Additionally, there is channeled advice from a Christmas angel whose only goal is to see you succeed in your journey.

Introduction

There are no reversals for these cards. If you do, however, choose to use them, it will be sufficient to use the meaning provided, and to add caution to the interpretation. For example, the Emperor card meaning begins with this: the Emperor knows what he wants, and he is very happy in the knowledge that his plans are sound and his methods are reliable. A reversal may suggest that though he knows what he wants, he's not quite sure that it's the right thing or that things will turn out. Still he remains confident, but cautious.

THE GHOSTLY PAST, PRESENT, AND FUTURE SPREAD

Many people already use this spread, and there's little to learn as far as the spread in general. The difference in this deck is that in addition to the card's general meaning, each card has a meaning for past, present, and future that applies to the card in the position where it lands. For example, using the Emperor meanings again:

The meaning in placement—that is, when it lands in one of the three past, present, and future spots in the layout—for the Emperor are:

Past: In the past, you may have had a really good plan and felt confident that you would succeed. And you did . . . unless you didn't. You instinctively know that answer as you pull this card. When you stuck to the plan, things most always went well. If a plan has not worked in the past, it's possible that because you were so accustomed to being right, you didn't even recognize the small flaw that tilted the axis. Stay calm, though; the future may surprise you. Keep to the plan.

Present: Pull out the "to-do list" as this is the only thing that will keep you on track right now. Everyone seems to need something from you: advice and solutions, wanting you to lead them, to follow your examples, etc. There are lots of pressures and many outcomes depending on you. Try to have as much confidence in yourself as others do.

Future: Planning for the future and controlling the outcomes is something you are great at doing. You've figured out the code to succeeding by standing tall, not giving in to fear, and manipulating things to your benefit. Manipulation is not as bad as it sounds because you are not the only one who will benefit from your efforts.

Introduction

Now, decide what question you'd like to delve into.
Lay three cards down in front of you.

Using the Emperor as example:

>Card 1: Past
>Card 2: Present
>Card 3: Future

The first card you've pulled is the Emperor. From the meanings prior: This is the **card 1 past** position. Read the past meaning from the meanings shown for the Emperor.

If the Emperor card fell instead in the middle slot, **card 2 present**, read the meaning for the present.

If the Emperor card fell in the third space, or **card 3 future**, read the meaning for the future.

You will note that each card has a Christmas element and that the guide will give you background or history on the image and what it may mean when seen in your reading. This is added interpretation to the supplied meanings and is very helpful to clarify the situation you are asking about.

Wild Card Questions: This deck lends itself well to having wild cards thrown into the mix. You have the three-card spread, and then you can add another clarifying card—or two or three—to address other things. Suppose in addition to the past, present, and future, you wanted to know about obstacles, or your strengths in the situation you'd inquired about, or what may be hidden from you? You can preassign extra spots to your three-card spread to answer anything you feel necessary. *

Finally there is a personal message to you that reflects the placement of the card in the form of a channeled Christmas angel message. At the onset of this project, I was given in meditation

Introduction

the message that the angelic force wished me to include personal messages from these very special holiday angels that provide what we call Christmas miracles, spirit, and love during the birth celebration of Jesus. I didn't know what to expect but sat, after prayer, at my computer and allowed the angels to take over. The messages were connecting and uplifting, reminding all of the love that occurs within this Christmas holiday for Christians, and others as well, who celebrate love throughout the year. In a reading, this message is particularly effective when things are less than promising or you need some solid ground. They give that push to rise up to the love available in the atmosphere. It allows one to "hang in there," "take the high road," and to generally "love thyself and thy neighbors."

> *** Wild Card Note:** You must assign the questions to the wild cards before you lay them down. Otherwise there's no way to know whether the powers that be are answering what you want them to or whether it's you "cherry-picking" your answers!

AN ORACLE, TOO

There are times that the traditional interpretations of the Tarot become overwhelming for readers, especially those new to it. There are many decks that strive to make the imagery more intuitive to read, but there are still issues with remembering the complexities. With this deck you will note that (as in some others) a keyword is shown to give the reader a push toward intuitive reading. Note too that the contemporary images give further clues as to how your personal life issues can be connected to the answers shown in the illustrations. Using the Emperor again, the keyword statement is Power. The general interpretation states that the Emperor knows what he wants and he is very happy in the knowledge that his plans are sound and his methods reliable. When you look at this more modern Emperor, do you see him thinking about his plans or is he looking at you, wondering how you will maintain your ideas or keep your power? Note that he has a journal and a pencil ready to put his mind to paper. Still, despite the firm ethics and fascinating reasoning, the ghost of the past screams. Could be good, could be bad. Either way, the indication is that your logic is of paramount importance.

When you look at the image, and if you didn't know the general meaning by heart, you would see a young man holding a pad of paper and a key statement telling you "power." He's making lists, or writing things down. He's making plans. There's a ghost screaming—or it seems to be. He has to be careful, right? He has to think things through and not be spooked by things. These ideas came from merely looking at the image. It really doesn't matter that this is the Emperor. He fits in the reading however the reader chooses.

Introduction

SAMPLE READING FOR
GHOSTS OF THE PAST, PRESENT & FUTURE

Example Situation/Question:
Tell me about my romantic life.

Card 1 Past: 2 High Priestess

In the past position this card could reflect the cycles of life. You've been on a path and you've had the knowledge (buried, but still there) that forward movement was about allowing yourself to listen to your heart. You've always known that you were where you were for a good reason—even if uncomfortable at times.

Card 2 Present: 0 Fool

Get on with it! You have places to go, people to meet, friends to make, and enemies to leave behind in your dust! It's time to recognize that you've already begun moving; your mind just hasn't gotten with the program. The whole idea is to put one foot in front of the other to move forward. It doesn't matter how slow you must go at this time. Just go. You can do it!

Card 3 Future: 16 Tower

The quicker you realize that one thing has now abruptly and explosively ended and that you need to stand up to the competition the better. It was bad. It was hurtful. It was needed. It's over. Stop crying the blues. At the end of a snowstorm, there's always a cleanup. Dig out.

Our interpretation: In the past our reader listened to her heart, even though it was uncomfortable. There was a good romantic match for the time. At her present she realizes that she needs to move on and leave this person. He is holding her back in some way. And finally, she is upset about leaving, but she recognizes the end, and now she has to pick up the pieces of a broken relationship.

THE MAJOR ARCANA

# The Major Arcana Cards

0 ~ FOOL

KEYWORD: *Beginning*

The Fool is on her way, and she starts this journey down a road less traveled and certainly unknown to her! She (or he!) clutches a bag that is filled with questions and unknown circumstances. She leaves behind measures of time, past images of places or interests, and future dreams of linear escapes as the newness she experiences moves forward, taking all the space within her soul for expanding growth. **Try to keep up.**

Christmas carols: In times past, Christmas carols were sung by those walking through the streets, drifting about the locales making sure that fires did not erupt within the cities, towns, and villages. These wandering minstrels could easily be seen as traveling singers, much like our Fool: a traveler with new songs to sing or words to learn. Sing loud, sing proud.

In a reading:

Past: You may have completed a journey in the past that was just part one of many to come. Is there something *now* that reminds you of *then*? Perhaps a lesson from your past is close by and will make this particular beginning both memorable and easier if you apply your learned—or unlearned—lessons.

Present: Get on with it! You have places to go, people to meet, friends to make, and enemies to leave behind in your dust! It's time to recognize that you've already begun moving; your mind just hasn't gotten with the program. The whole idea is to put one foot in front of the other to move forward. It doesn't matter how slow you must go at this time. Just go. You can do it!

Future: How did I ever come so far? you wonder. It's as though you've gotten to the place you are without ever realizing it. Look back briefly for any lessons or answers to questions that need to be packed into your bag of tricks. There's at least one that will do you well on the next part of your journey.

CHRISTMAS ANGEL MESSAGE

Don't get hung up on the details. Just love your family, your neighbors, and yourself as you travel.

1 ~ MAGICIAN

KEYWORD: *Energy*

The Magician is a very positive omen in the world of *A Christmas Tarot*. This wielder of power and energy can make something from nothing—or nothing from something. The idea is to keep the ideas on positive modes and not on the negative ones. The Magician looks deep within the self and in others before making decisions. **There is something to be accomplished.**

Christmas candy cane: This Christmas snack item originally was meant to keep those who should not speak quiet—children. The treat's popularity spread, and now trees sport them as decorations, and there is even a notion that the colors indicate the purity, Christ's blood, and the Holy Trinity. For this venue, we see a candy cane as a magic wand. When used correctly the individual is able to achieve goals, moving mountains if need be.

The Major Arcana Cards

In a reading:

Past: In the past, you've made the effort to begin anew and tried to remain positive as you pulled together something you thought was perfect. Of course, it was not, but you were still happy with it.

Present: Tweaking is required. It's not that things aren't going right; they are. But there are loose ends, and tying them up will make a very pretty package. Just don't let anyone else talk you out of your dreams.

Future: Hindsight is 20/20. Okay, so you left out a few important things when you were making your decisions. It's okay. For the most part, you hit the mark. The patient did not die.

CHRISTMAS ANGEL MESSAGE

Love transcends all beliefs and is the only magic you really need.

 The Major Arcana Cards

2 ~ HIGH PRIESTESS

KEYWORD: *Intuition*

The High Priestess knows without really knowing. Her intuition recognizes no bounds. She looks out over the world and offers that within each individual, going with the positive flow of things will eventually bring the soul to the light. She will dazzle those around her with psychic knowledge and implores you to stay on task. **Fame is coming for you! Go with the flow.**

Christmas gifts: One doesn't have to look far to consider the exciting reactions people feel when receiving a gift at Christmas. Though the more formalized tradition of gift giving didn't begin until the 1800s, there are stories around the world that include the exchange of gifts at this very special time from many cultures and time lines. Seeing a Christmas gift is very literal in this venue. You have or will receive a gift of some sort. Cherish it.

In a reading:

Past: This card could reflect the cycles of life. You've been on a path and you've had the knowledge (buried, but still there) that forward movement was about allowing yourself time to listen to your heart. You've always known that you were where you were for a good reason—even if you were uncomfortable at times.

Present: Look closely at the situation. You've moved into this spot purposely, and now you have had (or soon will have) a psychic knowing that will put you on solid ground. Listen! If you miss the cue, you could bring a negative twist to your future.

Future: The future is bright for this question—that is if you've listened to your own intuition. If you've allowed yourself to be subjugated, stop and stand up. Rethink things! If you are on the right path, you already know it. Keep cycling. Keep your doors open.

CHRISTMAS ANGEL MESSAGE

Know that gifts are not only for your own enjoyment: share the love.

The Major Arcana Cards

3 ~ EMPRESS

KEYWORD: *Productivity*

The Empress is the epitome of womanly influence and can be counted upon for lovely emotional discoveries and abundance of earthly passions. This centers on there being a time and place for everything and harvesting what you sow. Mindfulness benefits all. Being in touch both with nature and the physical world, there is productivity all around you in all the varied areas of mind, body, and spirit. **Something you've experienced in the past pays off.**

Poinsettia plant: The poinsettia plant blooms around Christmas time in Mexico and now can be found in other similar climates. It was there where people began to use it as a decoration—a plant that was only vivid in color at one season per year. Because of its beauty and growth plan, it's easy to see why it is relevant to the Earth to be displayed at a nurturing time of year.

The Major Arcana Cards

In a reading:

Past: This was a time when the seeds of your situation were planted. Maybe you planted them personally, or maybe someone else planted them in your name. Either way, understanding the desire was paramount and hopefully something that could be harvested from these particular seeds.

Present: You are in a growth spurt now, and preparing your way to the future by linking the past to the present is something that you've become good at. You put on your apron of creation and mix things (ideas) together to find the right solution for the problem or encounter.

Future: The pot roast is done! And it's Divine. The warmth exuded from your personality and your accomplishment welcomes those around you to celebration. It's time to dance!

CHRISTMAS ANGEL MESSAGE

Bloom in the knowledge that if you truly love another, you will be rewarded in ways you may not have thought.

 The Major Arcana Cards

4 ~ EMPEROR

KEYWORD: *Power*

The Emperor knows what he wants and he is very happy in the knowledge that his plans are sound and his methods reliable. When you look at this more modern Emperor, do you see him thinking about his plans or is he looking at you, wondering how you will maintain your ideas? Note that he has a journal and a pencil ready to put his mind to paper. Still, despite the firm ethics and fascinating reasoning, the ghost of the past screams. Could be good, could be bad. Either way, the indication is that your logic is of paramount importance. **You are on top for now.**

Letters to Santa: Writing a letter to Santa is an American tradition that began in the nineteenth century. The messages were a perfect barometer of the time and showed that ideas and issues were not wasted on the young. By reading them, an individual could understand the thoughts and desires of the writer. Want and reality mix.

In a reading:

Past: In the past, you may have had a really good plan and felt confident that you would succeed. And you did . . . unless you didn't. You instinctively know that answer as you pull this card. When you stick to the plan, things most always go well. If a plan has not worked in the past, it's possible that because you were so accustomed to being right, you didn't even recognize the small flaw that tilted the axis. Stay calm though, the future may surprise you. Keep to the plan.

Present: Pull out the "to-do list" as this is the only thing that will keep you on track right now. Everyone seems to need something from you: advice and solutions, wanting you to lead them, to follow your examples. There's lots of pressure and many outcomes depending upon you. Try to have as much confidence in yourself as others have in you.

Future: Planning for the future and controlling the outcomes is something you are great at. You've figured out the code to succeeding by standing tall, not giving in to fear, and manipulating things to your benefit. Manipulation is not as bad as it sounds, because you are not the only one who will benefit from your efforts.

CHRISTMAS ANGEL MESSAGE

It will be your job to decipher emotional difficulties with others, and then apply the love needed to bring the season into harmony with heaven's purpose.

5 ~ HIEROPHANT

KEYWORD: *Belief*

The Hierophant puts forth the beliefs that you hold dearly, and that by following your own moral fortitude, you will be able to see right from wrong. He knows the rules and abides by them when it is prudent to do so. If not, he is capable of analyzing the issues and applying intellect—even if it's something that disturbs daily life. Connect to your spiritual side; learn or understand what is before you. **Take the high road.**

Christmas rose: A European flower, the white Christmas rose (tipped with pink) blooms only in the winter. This lovely rose connects for many to the birth of Jesus and was a spiritual gift to the child from a poor shepherd girl. She was very sad that she had no gift to bring, but a special Christmas angel brought the flower from beneath the snow. The Christmas angel taught the young girl that love can bring forth a bloom of life that is also a true gift of the heart.

The Major Arcana Cards

In a reading:

Past: Your beliefs held you back for a while, and you had trouble coming to the right plan of action. Eventually, you found the answer within through relaxation, meditation, and identifying your true beliefs. You hoped that it was the right choice.

Present: There are new pros and cons that have come to light. There are shadows as well. More time is needed to analyze the situation. You might consider talking with someone you trust for their advice.

Future: Wow. How did that happen? While you're not sure things have happened exactly as you wanted, there are some real situations to think about now. All in all these are good developments, and you believe in yourself as never before. Relax; take a nap!

CHRISTMAS ANGEL MESSAGE

Believe in all ways of love and recognize the many ways to show it.

 The Major Arcana Cards

6 ~ LOVERS

KEYWORD: *Partnerships*

The Lovers card usually indicates a relationship between two individuals (possibly romantic, but could be otherwise); however, it's just as likely that the relationship could be directed inward to the duality of the self. There could be a difference of opinion or you may be having difficulty understanding the other part of an equation—the other person or your alter ego. Follow your own heart is the mantra of the day; just make sure you are considering all the facts, because your relationship could go wrong if you are not careful. **Look to an encounter with another that touches you deeply.**

Mistletoe: The perfect Christmas tradition for lovers (whether emotional or internal) is that of mistletoe. Early on, the Druids began its use in the forests during times of conflict. If one came upon the ball of mistletoe in the woods, all warring arms were put down, and a truce was called until the following day. It was in the eighteenth century when the kissing practice became of fashion and continues to this day.

In a reading:

Past: You may have had an interesting kind of relationship with someone in the past who made quite an impression, or you may be fairly impressed with your smart handling of a situation. Still, you really didn't look at the whole picture, and because of that, it's possible you've missed something. Too bad, it could make the future skewed.

Present: You feel as though you have a match made in heaven or that nothing in your life could go wrong. This could be the right thinking for you at present. Just be sure that the mirror you look into is not hiding ghosts from the past. If that's the case, take steps to bring things into the light.

Future: You are in line for a fabulous future as long as you've banished your demons! It seems that there is mistletoe wherever you go! Your relationships shine!

CHRISTMAS ANGEL MESSAGE

Loving others can be difficult, but doing it anyway is worth any inconvenience.

The Major Arcana Cards

7 ~ CHARIOT

KEYWORD: *Willpower*

A card of movement, the Chariot welcomes opposite energies coupled with the ability to solve struggles—if you're paying attention to what's in your own mirror image. There is victory in the crusade of this card—a balance of the cosmos as long as you're at the reins. **Move to rescue. Move to prepare. Move to the front of the line. Just move.**

Garland: Garland is a string of items hooked together and used for decorating Christmas trees or any part of a home or establishment during the winter season around the world. The festive drape came in to being as people working the land used their leftover foliage to sell in cords once the harvesting season was complete. Selling these lovely decorations allowed them the money to feed their families. It can represent hard work and moving forward as does the Chariot.

The Major Arcana Cards

In a reading:

Past: You've worked hard to get where you are. You've strived to keep moving forward and warded against slipping back into old patterns. Onward and upward!

Present: Things might seem scary or outside your control, but that's only an illusion or shadow. You are neck and neck with others, but they are not your adversaries as they support your journey as much as you recognize theirs. All is well, keep going; you're on the right track.

Future: Your final destination is right ahead, and you can see yourself firmly situated where you want to be. You're in charge of this good fortune; take a bow and then move on to the next challenge.

CHRISTMAS ANGEL MESSAGE

If you can survive it, you can learn from it.

 The Major Arcana Cards

8 ~ STRENGTH

KEYWORD: *Telepathy*

Instinct is high when this card is shown. Though animal communications are appropriate in thinking of the issues at hand, much more is at the crux: the simplistic interactions that spawn from that knowing place in your heart—your gut's urging. This is a calming card, but who is really at peace? The ghosts of your past or the feline that interprets intuition? **If the beast inside you speaks, listen!**

Nutcracker: Nutcrackers tend to look like soldiers (even when they depict another character), and they truly hold the representation of a soldier's job to protect and display power and a knowing. This German custom both of decoration and by traditionally used elements (they really do crack nuts) proposes the cycle of life, from the seed to the tree to humankind. Use inner strength and communications as well as outer control and knowledge.

In a reading:

Past: You've always known that you were in tune with nature and your fellow man and woman. This has always been a strength. Though there have been shadows from time to time trying to steal your resolve, you have always found your way. That light will always be there to guide you; use it.

Present: You feel as though you are on the same wavelength as someone else. There's a plan afoot, and you know that any partnership you forge will be successful because there will be a telepathic connection that is undeniable. Don't slack off. This is meant to be.

Future: You have been able to navigate through any number of situations merely by centering in on yourself and your ability to perceive the correct way of interacting with the world around you. Your strength is both inside and out. Smile and share your triumphs.

CHRISTMAS ANGEL MESSAGE

Knowing and understanding what others think can only act as a way to reduce the borders between beings.

9 ~ HERMIT

KEYWORD: *Truth*

It would seem that the Hermit is alone in the world, with only words from ghosts of the past to rely upon. Not so. The Hermit is just gathering the facts, putting them in formal arrangement, and preparing to storm the walls with new truths. This card speaks about those who are wise not only to worldly ways, but to the inner workings of destinies. There's more to be learned, however, and time to go before the light is seen at the end of the tunnel. **Focus on the joy shining down at this moment**.

Christmas wreath: In ancient times, it was thought that the wreath at Christmas was a symbol for victory. Though there are many other meanings for this lovely circle of nature, through the years and across customs, finding the inner truth was the theme. Seeing this wreath will signal that introspection of some sort will be needed; take the time to understand the situations from all sides. Then apply that knowledge.

The Major Arcana Cards

In a reading:

Past: During this time you sat back and collected data. It was uncomfortable to do so, but someone had to do it. You felt vindicated in having the best knowledge available; you will also be prepared to make the best decisions.

Present: You may feel you have a ghost on your back as you try to make the right decision. The ghost is just reminding you that you need to consider the facts you've gathered. You're tempted to disregard them because another course might be easier. Stop. Think. Then decide without emotional interference.

Future: You've done the work, made the adjustments, executed the plan, and now you can reap the rewards. It was a lonely trek in many ways, but sharp thinking has put you in a very good place.

CHRISTMAS ANGEL MESSAGE

Learn to recognize the truth and not to sugarcoat it.

 The Major Arcana Cards

10 ~ WHEEL

KEYWORD: *Luck*

The Wheel in many decks is the Wheel of Fortune; it involves luck, fortune, and change—and the reverses of each of those things. The Wheel is always moving in a circular fashion, and sometimes you are traveling through good times and sometimes bad. The idea is to keep your eyes peeled. If you are in a bad time, cheer up—good times are coming. If you are in good times, take heed of your surroundings and your ideas to stay on track—bad times are coming. **So, take a chance—or don't. Just be prepared.**

Christmas train: The train that moves in circles within a Christmas train garden keeps viewers in the mindset that things from the past continue to come 'round with comfort and constant movement. People think of this mostly as a remembrance of soldiers returning from war; the seeking of adventure and the comfort of return of loved ones over the years also come to mind. The journey around the track can help you understand that going from place to place on a train means that your life also moves in a circle of luck—and *not-so-much* luck. It goes 'round and 'round . . .

In a reading:

Past: Your luck changed, but which way depended upon how you judged a situation you were engulfed in. Either way, things are about to change again. So take what you know, keep it in the forefront of your mind, and prepare for the next windfall.

Present: You are in the thick of it. News, whether good or bad, is fleeting. Remember that there is a lesson to be learned right now. Though you don't mind retracing steps when they are good steps, you usually only are required to retrace *bad* steps. So enjoy if you can, and if not, take full heed so you don't have to run 'round the wheel again to land in this same place.

Future: Are you dizzy yet? Learning lessons can be exhausting, and it's often difficult to be prepared for every contingency. You're doing a good job, though. Keep at it. More good times are sure to grace you.

CHRISTMAS ANGEL MESSAGE

Minimize the stops at the negative outposts so that you can spend more time in the light.

11 ~ JUSTICE

KEYWORD: *Decisions*

Just as the pillow is thrown from the couch in this ghostly image, the Justice card makes evident the truths and puts them out there for all to see. Decisions must be made, and this is done by researching the case, thinking about outcomes, and balancing facts. **A verdict must be reached. Present your case.**

Cookies and milk for Santa: Leaving treats for Santa is a tradition that has found favor around the world, although kids leave many other things besides just milk and cookies! Everything from beer to wine and cookies to carrots (for the reindeer), and more, can be the "bribe" to the man in red. In the 1930s, children were schooled in the thought that giving was just as good as receiving, and though that lesson may be somewhat skewed today, we still hope that this is the outcome. Balance comes to mind.

The Major Arcana Cards

In a reading:

Past: It has not always been easy for you to be just in your thinking as it applies to the situation, and there's been some fear about the facts that could have been uncovered. Still, good or bad, research was required before a verdict could be considered. You've gotten all the facts you could. Stand tall in your knowledge.

Present: It's time to evaluate everything you've learned. Take a step back and look at the whole picture to see what jumps forth. Then you will have to gather everything you know before you make any decisions.

Future: All your good research will be put into place, and a decision—popular or unpopular—will be offered to you. Or possibly it will be you making the decision. Either way, feel pride in knowing that no mistakes were made, and you are serving justice.

CHRISTMAS ANGEL MESSAGE

Whether you like or dislike, if it is just, it must be objectively considered.

The Major Arcana Cards

12 ~ HANGED

KEYWORD: *Crossroads*

This card indicates a turning point. Think about the situation, improve it, think some more, and then choose the direction that will best help you succeed. It won't be an easy decision. It won't be a fast decision. And that decision comes with risks. This matters not, because once the decision is made, the hanged one is already working on what the next move will be. **Think about wearing stockings without holes.**

Christmas stocking: Just like the treats for Santa were given for a variety of reasons, stockings were hung near the chimney where Santa was known to visit through, carrying treats for him and the reindeer for their long trip. Later, this changed so that the stockings held treats for those within the household. Stockings remind one that surroundings can change according to the direction one walks. Don't worry about controlling the situation; instead trust yourself. The stocking holds the right treats for you.

In a reading:

Past: You've been tired and long for a rest. Figuring out situations and right methods has been so draining and difficult. You've taken to just hanging around and ignoring the crossroad. This didn't make the circumstances go away, though. Wake up please.

Present: You want to make a decision regarding which course to take, but there's that little doubt about choosing the wrong road. Fear not, both roads have their lessons; just try to make the best choice possible based on your exhaustive thinking about the situation.

Future: You have chosen a path that will take you directly to the outcome you've wanted. It may not be a clear passage, but when was that ever the case for you? Stifle your yawn and skip on down the road!

CHRISTMAS ANGEL MESSAGE

If you don't know which way to go, stand still. Wait for intuitive instruction.

The Major Arcana Cards

13 ~ DEATH

KEYWORD: *Change*

Under most circumstances, Death does not mean physical death, but rather a radical change in life (though there are circumstances that if correctly interpreted could mean a physical loss). This current time may require a difficult adjustment period, but it's all for the good—even if it may not seem so now. Don't resist it, whatever you do! Shielding yourself (or someone else) from this intense change will only cause more-serious issues. Grief must be gone through and then discarded before you can consider a new way of looking at the situation. **Stand up . . . right now . . . and take heart.**

Christmas bell: Christmas bells were traditionally rung just before Christmas mass, connecting the season with the clear sounds of a profound experience (good or bad). Now bells come in all sizes and decorative natures and tout a season full of ringing clarity. Bells also ring in the times of change and suggest that you look at things in a positive manner.

The Major Arcana Cards

In a reading:

Past: It may be that you've discovered you were at the very end of something. It may not have felt like a good thing, but you knew somewhere in your being that there would be a positive outcome down the road. Keeping your chin up would have been the best way to handle the downpour of unusual circumstances—one hopes that you were optimistic. If not, well, it was what it was. Onward and upward.

Present: Now that you are in the crux of change, it still may feel uncomfortable, but at least you can see the path and recognize that, though maddening, you can take the right road to recovery. If you choose the wrong approach, though, it could lengthen your stay in discomfort. Keep your eye on the prize despite the zombie-like undead at your back.

Future: You have come through difficult times and are now on the other side of pain (emotional or physical). You feel scarred and tired, but now you can move forward toward a good, stable environment. Don't forget what has occurred, though, because that knowledge can be put in your toolbox of things to remember for the next time. Yes . . . there's always a next time. Listen for the bell.

CHRISTMAS ANGEL MESSAGE

Wake up. You may think you are dead. You are not.

The Major Arcana Cards

14 ~ TEMPERANCE

KEYWORD: *Dynamics*

This is the card of creativity and of making something from nothing. It indicates a time of personal growth and understanding of the self and others. Environments (situations and actual places) can be changed now by considering what you have at your fingertips. You may not even recognize the tools in your toolbox, but they are there. If there was ever a "MacGyver" card, this one is it! **Look for your miracle!**

Angel: Angels have always been known as messengers from God and can be found in most religions around the world. Tales and encounters are countless, and the Christmas angels are the most popular in their long history because of their assistance in events before, during, and after the birth of Christ. Wise creatures, they are said to know all except what can be changed by humans applying their will or things that God alone knows. They are peaceful, balanced, and understanding of their places in the universe. This is the goal of the Temperance as well.

In a reading:

Past: You've had to clean up a mess of some kind, and you've accomplished it with grace and finesse. With your stable thinking and kind advice, you followed your spirit into the battle with strength and love. This could have been a personal inside-the-self disaster or something coming at you or yours from the outside—no matter; you did the right thing. Don't doubt yourself.

Present: Keep your calm. Think things through. Don't fall into the traps of those around you who may not see the big picture. Keep your thoughts pure and your mind humming along at moderate speed. You have an angel on your shoulder, and that's the very best sign that you are on the right track.

Future: You've solved the problem; now stop and rest. The situation may not be entirely over, but you've nothing to worry about. You have several possibilities open to you now, and it will be your job to objectively use all you've learned and to choose the best method to get what you need.

CHRISTMAS ANGEL MESSAGE

Keep your mind clear and your eyes on the road ahead. That way you will avoid potholes.

15 ~ DEVIL

KEYWORD: *Entrapment*

Not usually a good card, the Devil indicates a trap—and one that is not easily maneuvered. The worst of it is that you've probably already seen the trap, have stepped into it, and cannot see a way out. You've lost your belief in yourself. Even if there *is* a way out (a small one to be sure), you won't believe it's for you. The old Murphy's Law statement, "If something *can* go wrong, it will" is the mantra for the Devil. **Broken promises steal your resolve; get out while you still can, if you still can.**

Coal: The Italian witch La Belfana and Austria's Krampus both have the same rumblings of creation regarding the giving of coal at Christmas. Do bad; get bad. Then enjoy coal in your stocking. This goes way back, and parents for many moons have used the stories, they hope, to bring a child to do good throughout the year. The connection to the Devil card is merely the knowledge that traps you lay for others could be hidden throughout *your* time here, and that you may eventually step into them yourself.

The Major Arcana Cards

In a reading:

Past: Okay, now you've done it. Was that quicksand you stepped into? Whatever it was, something has happened (of your own making most likely) that you are horrified by—or at the very least guilty of. Nothing to do now but take your lumps and see what happens. It's okay, not everyone drowns . . . start over with better thinking next time.

Present: You're digging a deep hole and the rain is filling it up—with you inside. Look around quickly and make whatever decision you can to get out of the predicament—without hurting someone else. As soon as you drag someone down with you, the ante is upped in the negative. You already have enough problems. Be smart! Think again.

Future: There's nothing to do except get up and dust yourself off. Make amends to anyone you've damaged with your poor decisions. Everyone makes mistakes, but this one will be a doozy if you don't wake up to the consequences of your wrong thinking or doing.

CHRISTMAS ANGEL MESSAGE

You're in the wrong. Do right by yourself and others. Now.

 The Major Arcana Cards

16 ~ TOWER

KEYWORD: *Electricity*

Electrical impulses are indicated when the Tower card shows. These impulses can be good or they can be bad. You might have an idea that electrifies the world or just you. But more often than not, the shocking allure to this card is not a good thing—something has usually gone terribly awry in the Tower. You can't see your way through the storm. There's no way out of a bad situation. You feel helpless in this sour circumstance. There is hope, however. **Address your beliefs and make lemonade quickly.**

Snowman and snow: Snow at Christmas. Building a snowman. Snow in general. Lovely to look at but sometimes disastrous. Though it can show the beginning of a winter season, as it melts it can indicate an end. It seems that snow brings to mind different things to different people. Just like the Tower. Will there be thundersnow, or will you build a happy snowman once the snow has stopped? It makes a difference.

In a reading:

Past: Something has happened that has shocked you to the core. You may not know how to go on or what decisions to make that will cause things to go back to the way they were. Hopefully, you recognized that going back was not a likely possibility and did not waste too much time thinking about it.

Present: Everything around you is falling down—could be literal, could be figurative. Doesn't matter; there may be a storm that envelops your very being. What you do and how you do it will be the difference between making progress or wallowing in the muck. Try not to wallow for too long.

Future: The quicker you realize that one thing has now abruptly and explosively ended and that you need to stand up to the competition, the better. It was bad. It was hurtful. It was needed. It's over. Stop crying the blues. At the end of a snowstorm, there's always a cleanup.

CHRISTMAS ANGEL MESSAGE

You can fly. You've forgotten that, but you can.

17 ~ STAR

KEYWORD: *Hope*

It may be a surprise to you, but you are seen by those around you as a rising star—could be emotionally or because of the positive direction you are always heading. You are growing and living up to your highest goals, and you certainly know what you are talking about. **It's your time. That's right; walk the walk, star child!**

Christmas star: Most people think of the Star of Bethlehem when the Christmas star is mentioned. It acted as a guide to wise men who were to witness a spectacular event. Others still feel the star connection, however, because the skies and the bodies within are there for all of us to draw faith from.

The Major Arcana Cards

In a reading:

Past: You came, you saw, you conquered. Yes, you were the shining light within your soul and for those around you as well. Eventually, though, you knew you would move along and would need a sturdy rope to pull the star along with you.

Present: Bask in the light. Celebrate. Give thanks. You know what you want, are close to getting it (or you may already have recently been blessed), or have charted your course. Keep on the same track. Follow your star.

Future: Your star is always with you deep inside your soul, reminding you that this decision was the right one, and you are heading in the right direction. You've come a long way to find yourself here—not with just one star, but many. Smile; life will be good for some time to come.

CHRISTMAS ANGEL MESSAGE

Remember that a star is only as bright as those watching it. Or you.

 The Major Arcana Cards

18 ~ MOON

KEYWORD: *Hidden*

The Moon is about continuing cycles and invites people to follow their instincts. These inner knowings are oftentimes mysterious, but nonetheless a great way to nudge the impulses that come so readily to you. There may be impulsive thinking or unstructured time frames when this card shows its face, but those are good implements for developing your intuitive abilities. Use them. **Watch carefully: As you go down the steps to your inner self, there could be a psychic moment.**

Christmas candles: The flickering lights of candles are something that has been passed down through the ages by many cultures. The Romans offered them to the god of Saturn because the planet was symbolic of light. With the onset of Christianity, candles have been placed in windows to guide visitors (at one time to guide the wise men to the Christ child), and Victorians placed them on trees as a symbol of the "original" star. But the light is not bright when the Moon is involved. Hold the candle, but have your intuition handy.

In a reading:

Past: You've kept your cards close to the vest as you've moved through this situation. Silence, introspection, and inner discoveries were the tasks of the day. You needed to consider things carefully and fully. It's not that you were afraid of making a wrong decision. You just wanted that decision to be the very best one for your growth. You did well, my friend.

Present: Whether a wolf howls at the moon or monks retreat to their places of worship, pondering the light and how it affects each part of your situation requires solidarity. Things could be buried in your subconscious that need to be brought to light and considered. You are intuitive, so it will be a good thing. Just don't let the true face of your burdens scare you. You're strong in your nature.

Future: You've made your decisions on the basis of the very best knowledge you had, and you will continue to explore your inner self to find ways to make things even better. Going through seemed like a long journey when you were there, but now, looking back, it was but a snip of time. And you and your intuitive ability to peek behind the curtain and take the stairs in two steps at a time make a bright future.

CHRISTMAS ANGEL MESSAGE

Shadows are muddy only for as long as you do not shine your light.

The Major Arcana Cards

19 ~ SUN

KEYWORD: *Freedom*

The Sun card offers all kinds of freedom: living an independent life, acting as a free spirit, and young at any age. It's a nurture-and-nature card that offers a hope and love to everyone in its path. You're getting your way, trying new things, embracing the bold ideas. **Success is in your path. You can't miss it.**

Christmas tree: The Christmas tree has roots of many sorts, including one that reminds us that pagans have always used evergreens inside the home during the winter solstice. There is controversy for any specific beginning—some say Germany, Latvia, and others—mostly around the 1500s. People today even argue about its appropriateness in places. No matter, for those who relish the tradition of decorating a Christmas tree, the joy and benefits of nature and its beauty cannot be denied. Love, growth, rejoice! It's a sunny time!

The Major Arcana Cards

In a reading:

Past: What a great time it was and how well you handled yourself in all your life plans. Having fun was a good way to start, and you will strive to continue in that fashion. Success was visible, and you were running toward it full speed.

Present: Rally round the Christmas tree and bask in the lights (from the tree, from within, and from the sun!). This is your time to shine. Whatever you are planning or thinking, it is within your means to accomplish it. Even if the idea is half baked, it will still work. But the better your idea, the better the outcome. Think big!

Future: You can relax a bit and enjoy the fruits of making good decisions, having great outcomes, or being part of a team that is on the winning side. You can afford to give to others now, for you've gained so much in your sunshine. Emotional and material items are still within your grasp if you desire them.

CHRISTMAS ANGEL MESSAGE

Individual desires power the masses. Make your light's fuel as strong as you can.

 The Major Arcana Cards

20 ~ JUDGMENT

KEYWORD: *Outcomes*

The Judgment card gives an uncomfortable message. It indicates that difficult outcomes are at hand about something important in your life. Waiting for those results to come down is the challenging part. Prayers go up, cases are presented, and other forms of worry abound. Remember, though, that it's always how you react to a decision that counts. Communications in the right manner can help, but know that your destiny is at stake here. **There could be a surprise; think before you speak.**

Holly: It was believed by the Druids that holly was a part of the Earth that was meant to keep it beautiful when foliage lost leaves during the winter months. But oddly, it has also come to represent peace, and there were those in the past who settled disputes beneath a holly tree. Another component in a story talks of the holly giving heed to who in the house (he or she) would rule the home the following year.

In a reading:

Past: Why is it that you are always the one forced to make the hard decisions? It doesn't seem fair, but judgment of you has always been in the center. You've gotten through most of it; just having a good attitude has helped you immeasurably. One foot in front of the other was all you could accomplish.

Present: Remember you can make great outcomes as well as the others who seem to be judging you. Think of the self now, carefully put your case together, then make the best of what the circumstances have supplied you. Ultimately, the only person responsible for the outcome of a situation you are in—or you (directly or indirectly)—is you.

Future: You come through the situation knowing that whatever decisions or judgments you've made, they were the best that could have been achieved. Could the outcome have been more positive? Yes, but that's the case with most decision making. You did well. Don't overthink it.

CHRISTMAS ANGEL MESSAGE

Stand firm. You know what's right. Discard the rest.

The Major Arcana Cards

21 ~ WORLD

KEYWORD: *Completion*

The World completes the Fool's journey and begins the process of rebirth and reincarnation. You can take a breath now because something has completed, and now you will be able to move forward to a new situation or encounter. Consider what you have learned about the situation or person in question. This will give you a heads-up about what to do or not to do the next time. **Fresh start.**

Manger or Nativity scene: The manger or the Nativity scene of course depicts the birth of the Christ child and the day we call Christmas. It is said that St. Francis of Assisi in Italy brought the nativity to life when he felt people (over 800 years ago) had forgotten the meaning of Christmas. It asks us to reflect on the past, evaluate the present, and project love into the future.

The Major Arcana Cards

In a reading:

Past: Moments of the past may have seemed scary or difficult to manage. There were always too-many others or things getting in the way of your thinking. But by keeping your head and considering all sides of every issue laid before you, you were able to sleep at night. You have come full circle. You knew what not to do, as well as the true path.

Present: The world is your oyster now. You can take a sigh of relief knowing that whatever has happened is over, and you are the better for it. If you don't feel the better, stop and rethink it until you come to that conclusion. You don't want to carry any negativity over to the next situation.

Future: Learning the lessons you needed to make it to completion was imperative and you passed with flying colors. Any inkling of negativity has been dispelled and you've managed to learn most of what was made available. Do you have to "go through" again? Of course you do, silly! That's life!

CHRISTMAS ANGEL MESSAGE

Rest on your seventh day. You've worked hard.

WHAT IF YOU WANT MORE THAN A 3-CARD SPREAD?

This deck, though specifically created to work alongside the scary ghosts in the Dickens classic, can be utilized with any spread used with any other Tarot or oracle deck: including the 5-, 7-, and 9-card spreads, the Celtic Cross, and any number of layouts that you might create on your own.

You will note that on the first page of each card description there is a basic card meaning that follows closely to traditional Tarot meanings. On the final page of the card description, there is a Christmas angel message. These can be used with any spread to accomplish longer, more-detailed readings. You can even include the Christmas item description in your reading as you consider the ghostly images. Using other spreads with this deck allow you to go behind the simplistic 3-card, past, present, future offerings. Additionally, though we don't use reverses with this treatment and, as mentioned early on, they can be used if you choose. Just take the upright meaning and add a caution. For example, when you read the upright Judgment card to say "think before you speak," the reversed caution would be: "Just don't *over*think it."

We've provided three additional spreads here for you to consider beyond the ghostly past, present, and future!

The Major Arcana Cards

The Christmas Cross

Card 1: The person, question, or situation you wish to concentrate on.

Card 2: How you got to this place. The past. What happened that made the situation begin or explode.

Card 3: What has just happened.

Card 4: What could happen next.

Card 5: What could happen in the future if things do not change.

A Christmas Career

For this spread, each 2-card grouping should be read together as one message. So if your first two cards were the Judgement card (meaning think before you speak) and the Tower (make lemonade), you might take the first pairing regarding what happened to you to mean that you were not in a good position. You needed to keep quiet, think things through, and do the best you could with what you had. Something not so nice was coming for you! How you handled your attitude was what brought you to the present.

Cards 1 & 2: What has happened to you that you need a new job? What have you learned in the past that will help you find a new position? Why are you looking for a position, or what efforts can you take from your past to help you in your search?

Cards 3 & 4: What's going on now?

Cards 5 & 6: What will the outcome be?

Cards 7 & 8: What can you do to improve your future?

The Major Arcana Cards

Christmas Love Box

Card 1: What am I looking for in a mate?

Card 2: What do I have to offer a mate?

Card 3: What obstacles will there be?

Card 4: What is my next step?

Card 5: Tell me about my mate.

WRAPPING UP

When Charles Dickens took readers through the ghosts of past, present, and future, it was to teach a lesson. This deck too strives to teach each of us that not only is Christmas a religion of Christianity, but that religions and customs around the world have been melded together to offer the message of peace and love today. Let your past, present, and future allow you to grow in the love available in true humanity. It's there to see, if you would just look.

We hope you've enjoyed this Fool's Journey through our ghostly deck, and invite you to learn as we did, and continue on with those lessons. And finally, we hope you love this deck's premise enough to share it with others as it has been infused with positive light by your Christmas angels!

With love and light,
Dinah Roseberry and Christine "Kesara" Dennett

RESOURCES

The following Internet references were used to research the varied meanings for the Christmas elements shown in this deck:

https://festivenativities.com
www.christmascarnivals.com
www.christmastreehistory.net
www.familychristmasonline.com
www.magicofnutcrackers.com
www.proflowers.com
www.reference.com
www.smithsonianmag.com
www.thehistoryofchristmas.com
www.whychristmas.com

ABOUT THE AUTHOR & ILLUSTRATOR

DINAH ROSEBERRY

Dinah Roseberry has been writing for a living for many years. She is a senior editor for Schiffer Publishing's Paranormal/Mind, Body, Spirit/UFO lines and began channeling Light Beings in 2006. An author of books and boxed sets for Schiffer, she also finds time to write romantic intrigue, sci-fi, fantasy, horror, and even poetry. She is the founder of the UFO Management Group.

Dinah is also a practicing certified hypnotist with her practice centering on past-life regression, alien abductions, and other paranormal topics. She reads the Tarot and varied oracles as well and finds that divination often relaxes her in ways only her soul can identify. Her books and decks include: *First Light Tarot*, *Ghost Hunters' Tool Kit*, *Psychic Pets: Solving Paranormal Mysteries*, and *UFO and Alien Management: A Guide to Discovering, Evaluating, and Directing Sightings, Abductions, and Contactee Experiences*. For more information about Dinah, her books, and activities, visit www.roseberrybooks.com.

CHRISTINE "KESARA" DENNETT

Christine "Kesara" Dennett early on displayed an unusual ability to perform "psychic drawings," discovering she could intuitively see and illustrate unseen or future events. This first occurred as a teenager when she illustrated a portrait of her future husband. In her twenties she met him. At first she thought this was a remarkable coincidence until she later had children and found previous illustrations of them. Throughout her life, she experienced numerous ET, psychic, and ghostly encounters, forever establishing her connection to the paranormal realms.

Christine grew up and pursued a formal artistic education. During that same time she became Buddhist and received the ordained name of "Kesara." She used the name to represent her love and devotion toward art.

In 1986, Christine began working with prominent UFO researchers and parapsychologists with their investigations into UFO and ghost encounters. After thirty-one years of illustrating more than 300 renderings of actual events, Christine has perfected her ability to tune into the mind of a witness or the psychic imprint of an event. Her reputation as a "psychic artist" is now world renowned. She has worked with more than a dozen researchers on books, documentaries, and television shows.

Christine "Kesara" Dennett currently resides in Oregon with her husband, daughter, and grandson enjoying nature and family. Visit her website at: www.kesara.org.